MEET THE
SCHOOL NURSE

Written and Illustrated by

MARJORIE PICARD, R.N.

To order additional copies of this book, contact:
Xlibris
844-714-8691
www.Xlibris.com
Orders@Xlibris.com

ISBN: Softcover   978-1-4363-1426-8
           EBook   978-1-4771-7375-6

Print information available on the last page

Rev. date: 02/28/2022

To my always-supportive husband,

OTTO PICARD

NURSE'S
OFFICE

What, you might ask,
does the school nurse do?

She's here to help
and take care of you.

She gives you
a bandaid for
that scratch
on your knee,

She
gives
you
an
ice
pack
if
you
run
into
a
tree

She calls your mom
if your fever is high,

And gives you a hug if a
pain makes you cry.

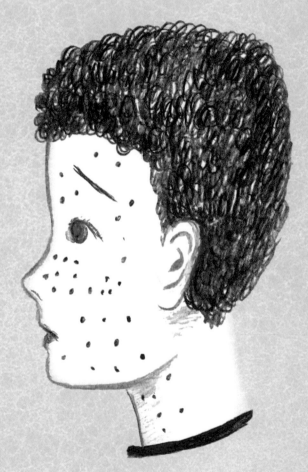

She looks at your skin
and sometimes sees

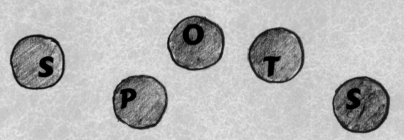

And into your hair for
bugs small as dots.

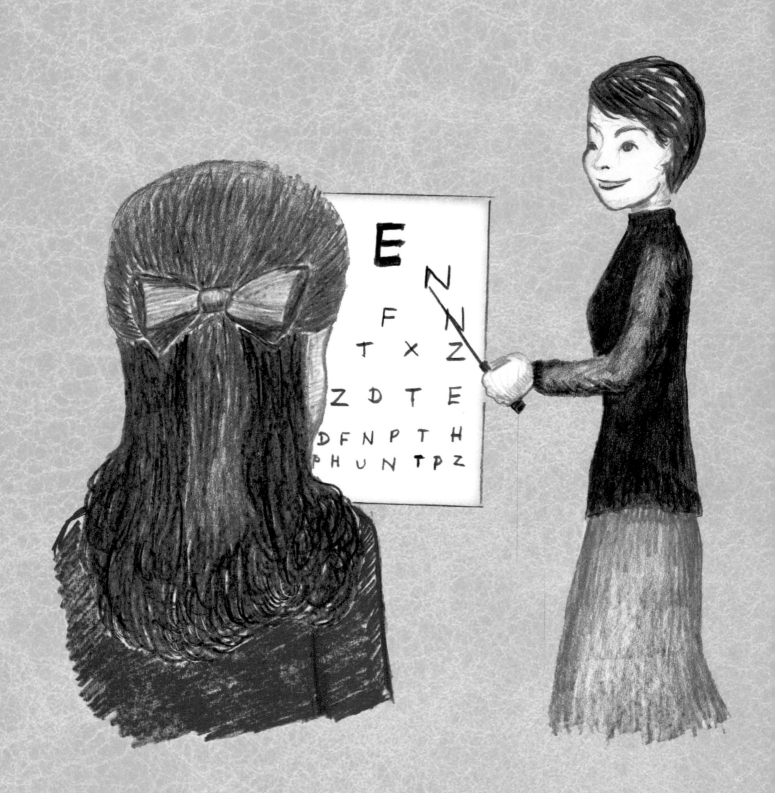

With a shape or a letter
she checks out your eyes,

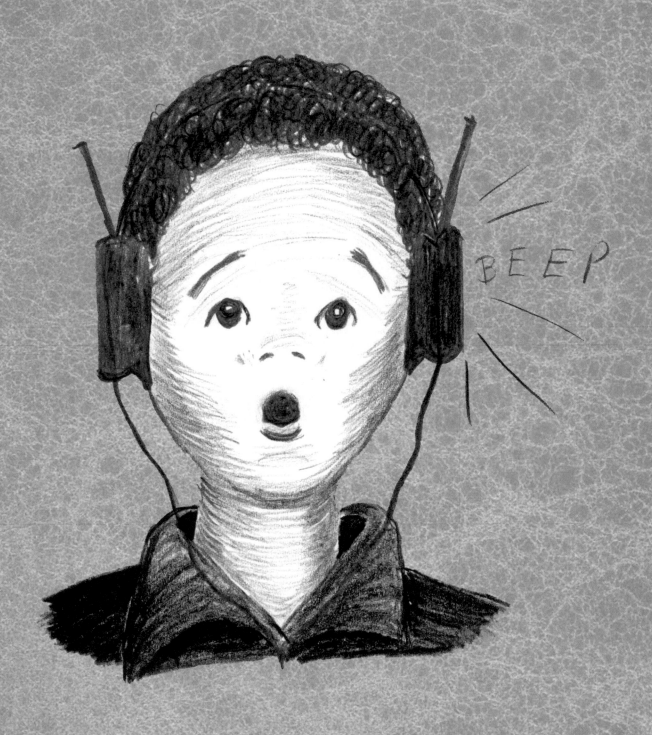

And makes "beeps" in your ears, sometimes a surprise.

She measures your weight in pounds and in ounces,

And your height on that scale that wiggles and bounces

The nurse wants you
happy and healthy, it's true,

She is your friend
and is there just for you.

Printed in the United States
by Baker & Taylor Publisher Services